Don't Block Your Bloom

I am Powerful!

By Mary Gerald-Patterson

Hey my sista, I pray that this book finds your hands at the perfect time. I want to remind you of how powerful you are and how much the world needs the gift that you carry. I pray that you are empowered.

Love & Light

Mary Patter

Printed in the United States of America

First Printing, 2019

ISBN 978-0-578-50926-6

www.Dontblockyourbloom.com

Table of Contents

DEDICATION

With love, peace, and hope, I dedicate this book:

❖ To anyone who has a story to share, anyone who has gone through things that you thought would break you, anyone who has lost battles, and has lost and found yourself.

❖ To my sisters and brothers who are working hard to heal themselves from past mistakes, break generational curses, and abuse of any kind.

LETTER FROM THE AUTHOR

Thank you for supporting my book. My prayer is that this book found your hands at the perfect moment, and that you are truly blessed by it. Make sure you stay connected and don't forget to send me your testimony after reading. Now! I cannot start this book without first stating my testimony, so that you know I am a living testament to all you are about to read. Here is a little bit about me. Enjoy!

With love, light, and hope,

Mary Gerald-Patterson

 *LOST*

Having gone astray or missed the way;
bewildered as to place & direction.

If you are, or were, anything like me, there was a stage in your life during your teenage years where you thought you had life figured out, and believed you were grown enough to know a little more than your parents or guardian(s). For me, this age was 16. The older generations may tell you that you're "smelling yourself." If you can't relate to this stage of life, keep reading. I'm sure you'll relate to something else along the way. Anyway, I was 16, and certainly in the process of finding myself. On this quest, I started to explore my sexuality and began showing interest in other females. During my time in high school, this lifestyle was easy to "fall" into, and soon, as the word hit the halls, the floodgates had opened. It was something about this lifestyle that was very enthralling, and before I knew it, dating females became seven years of my life. There was one particular woman that had a dangerous hold on me. I met her at a local festival, and it was lust at first sight—we became friends first, and then lovers. Of course, my mother did not approve of my lifestyle; she is a God-fearing woman, and this was not what she wanted or envisioned for her daughter. My lifestyle choices created a strain on our relationship, to say the least. I felt that my mom was angry with me, disappointed, and embarrassed. My choices had certainly caused friction between the two of us. Eventually, I decided to move out of my mother's house and in with my then girlfriend. I finally felt free to be who I wanted to be.

At this point, my mother and I barely spoke. She didn't know where I lived and some days, she wondered if I were dead or alive. This disconnection from my mother created an empty space in me that only my mother could fill. I carried on as if none of this mattered or affected me. My relationship with my girlfriend was exciting, carefree, and fun until we realized that we were both alpha females who never wanted to back down and were unconsciously fighting for the "alpha" position in the relationship. As you can imagine, this became quite dysfunctional and grounds for all types of negative outcomes. I totally lost myself in this relationship. I became dangerously controlling, and one day, I decided if my words couldn't penetrate, if I put my hands on you, you would understand what I was trying to say. Yes, I became the abuser, and that was not a good idea. Things really became bad, and as I said earlier, I totally lost myself and the relationship was breeding toxic behaviors from us both. About five years into the relationship, we decided to go our separate ways. We knew it would be best for both of us. We remained friends because we were better off that way.

After this relationship ended, I continued to date more to "have fun." I missed my mother during this time, and I'm sure she missed me too! I knew I'd caused her a lot of disappointment, worry, and heartache; a part of me just wanted my mother. I started to think, "Maybe if I dated men, I would make everyone happy, especially my mother." I met this charming guy who had a bad boy streak to him. For some reason, I was attracted to "bad boys"—the guys I knew damn well I should not be dating. This particular guy was nice, charismatic, and showered me with gifts and attention. We ran the streets and had a good time together. A good time was all I really cared about, who doesn't want a good time in their 20s? Some months into our friendship/relationship, I said something he did not like and his hand came flying across to the passenger seat where I was sitting. All I could think was…Did he just hit me? Yes, he did! This was a red flag that I ignored; I was comfortable with dysfunctional relationships. He was not only testing me to see if this was a behavior I would allow, but he was also showing me who he really was. I should have listened to my intuition and left at that very moment. I should have run for my life, but I didn't! For him, my stay was consent that I was okay with being smacked around and treated like anything. A year or so into the relationship, I became pregnant with my first child. I was happy, as any new parent would be, but the abuse and dysfunction didn't stop. In fact, it grew more frequent, and still I did not leave. Sad to say, I had become immune to the verbal, physical, and mental abuse that developed in the relationship.

About seven months into my pregnancy, I received a call from my ex-girlfriend, the one I mentioned to you earlier. She asked me how I was doing and if I still loved her, and told me that she wanted to try again. I told her that I didn't love her in that way anymore, and that we shouldn't entertain the idea of getting back together, because I was pregnant and in a relationship. Those words broke her heart; I could feel and hear the heartbreak in her voice. Three days later, I received a call from her best friend informing me that she had died from a seizure. My heart was broken. A part of me still loved her, but I couldn't tell her that. At the end of it all, she was still a friend that I knew would do anything for me, and I loved her dearly because of it. Regret started to set in—regret that I did not tell her I still loved her, and regret that I couldn't be there for her. She died completely alone; she was not found until three days after her death. How do you grieve the loss of an ex while in a current relationship? In this case, you don't! It was grounds for more arguments and dysfunction. I moved on, got over it, and bottled it up. I felt like my world was rolling down a hill of so many emotions. There I was eight months into my pregnancy, and no one knew what I was dealing with.

On top of that, I was too ashamed to discuss the abusive relationship, and too far gone to get out, so I thought. In the midst of it all, I managed to hold on to the joy of becoming a mother. Now, nine months pregnant and one week from my due date, as a new mother-to-be, I was excited and anxious to meet my beautiful baby girl. The doctors told me she was healthy and growing perfectly; her room was set up, and my bags were packed for the hospital. On December 16, 2008, I woke up and my stomach was a little tight; it felt like the baby was balled up and comfortable. I went to work, and around my lunch hour, I noticed she hadn't changed positions in a while. I drank a cup of cold apple juice in hopes to shake her up a little—it usually did, but that didn't work this time. At that point, I started to worry. The unknown was becoming a little unnerving. I called my doctor, and he told me to come into the office. Thank God that I was only ten minutes away from the doctor's office. I arrived, and they immediately hooked me up to the Doppler Ultrasound device to monitor the baby's heartbeat. Hearing her heartbeat relieved some of the worries that I was feeling, but she still wasn't moving. I sat attached to this machine for about an hour. The doctor started to become concerned because she still hadn't moved and that may be a sign of distress. I was instructed to go to the hospital where I was scheduled to deliver—to ensure the baby's safety. That brief moment of relief that I had was now completely gone. It was prayer time!

The unknown at this point frightened me; I didn't know what to think. I had to drive myself to the hospital which was about 40 minutes away from where I was. I had 40 minutes to pray, worry, and pray some more. I arrived at the hospital; the nurse and the doctors were waiting for my arrival. They immediately connected the heart monitor around my belly, trying to find the baby's heartbeat. I knew something was wrong because it was taking the nurse too long to locate the baby's heart. The doctor then suggested that we do an ultrasound to see the baby. A second doctor was called to examine the ultrasound, they both looked at me with the bad news eyes, and that is when I heard, "Ms. Gerald, I am so sorry, there is no heartbeat." They pointed to the heart chamber on the ultrasound monitor, and there sat a lifeless heart—the heart of the baby I nurtured and carried for nine months! At that moment, my soul left my body. The room was closing in on me. I couldn't hear. All I felt was pain—the pain of death, emotional pain, and sorrow. I wanted to die! I had absolutely no desire to live. Neither my mind nor my heart could comprehend what I just heard. My entire world just came down on me! I began sobbing and pleading with the doctors to give me a C-section and try to save her.

There was nothing they could do because her heart had already stopped beating and a C-section was not an option. Forced to birth her as if she were alive, I faced a degree of suffering that you wouldn't grasp without experience. I went through labor, waited to dilate 10cm to push, all while bawling and trying to understand the fact that my baby would not be alive when I birthed her. This beautiful baby girl that I would never see grow into a beautiful woman, that I would never have a chance to nurture. She was 7pd.5oz. and perfect to me. I held her in my arms and wept until the nurses came and took her away. A day later, I was discharged from the hospital, leaving without my child, empty arms, empty car seat, and an empty crib. I was broken, lost, and felt so alone. I was angry as hell. I wouldn't wish this type of pain on anyone. My mother planned a beautiful homegoing service for my baby girl. I have never seen a casket so small. This was the hardest thing I ever had to face in my life. After the funeral, I went to my mother's house and stayed in the basement. As the days passed, depression started to set in, and I was still in a dysfunctional relationship. I know you are thinking, Wow! You're still with this guy? Yes, I was.

Months after the death of my daughter, I was overcome with joy and gratitude to find out I was pregnant again. I was happy and scared at the same time. I was focused on doing all that I could to make sure this baby was healthy and safe; Lord knows I couldn't take another tragedy. I remembered getting into an argument with my boyfriend, and as I was walking away, trying to avoid the confrontation, I was kicked in the back. At that moment, I remember telling myself, "If you fight back, this baby will not make it, just walk away." When the time came, I birthed a beautiful baby who was only four pounds and in the Neonatal Intensive Care Unit (NICU). I finally got out of the abusive relationship and started to raise my child. At 25 years old, I felt lost, broken, and still ignorant of who I was. I thank God for a mother who loved me unconditionally and never stopped praying for me. I know her prayers saved me. She was there to help me figure it all out.

 # BROKEN

Interrupted, disrupted, or disconnected:
weakened in strength, spirit, etc.

Life has taken me for a whirlwind, and honestly, there have been times when I couldn't see myself recovering from it, emotionally or mentally. My Broken state became my normal. I became comfortable in it, and I was secretly suffering. Well, at least I thought I was secretly suffering. My broken spirit was apparently visible to others who were also broken; it was something in me they could identify with. Not understanding how to protect my spirit, energy, or space, I allowed them into my space which prohibited me from realizing how "broken" I really was— mindlessly trying to feed their broken state when I had nothing to pour from my own cup. I never allowed my "friends" around my child, and that says a lot. I knew that I needed to get tired of me, tired of the repeated behavior and realize that it's no longer about me, but the innocent child that was depending on me to get my life in order.

As a single mother, I was attracting dysfunction. I still had not faced the healing process that needed to take place from the death of my child or the abuse I endured. I was desperately trying to figure out who I was, why I was so angry at the world, and how to heal from the years of mental, physical, and emotional abuse. My spirit was broken, my heart was in pieces, and my thoughts were disorganized. This load was heavy, and I needed to get tired of carrying it and start unpacking it. I knew if I wanted different, I had to do something different. I was looking outwardly for something that could only be found inward; nobody was coming to save me from myself. I had to choose to save myself, and that was easier said than done.

Affirmations

I will boldly face the issues that are holding me in a place of brokenness.

I have the power to save myself.

I will be intentional about my wholeness.

I deserve to be whole and happy.

I will release myself from_____

Scriptures to pull from:

Jeremiah 30:17: But I will restore you to health and heal your wounds; declares the LORD...

Psalm 147:3: He heals the brokenhearted and binds up their wounds.

Write your own affirmations:

_____

_____

_____

_____

_____

_____

_____

_____

_____

_____

_____

_____

_____

_____

_____

_____

_____

_____

_____

# FACE IT

No longer denying or ignoring...

I was hiding from myself, hiding from the pain I buried within—the emotional pain that physically manifested into anger, insecurity, bitterness, and regret. There was nothing for me in this place—my soul yearned to be free. You can't run from yourself forever, and I was running a marathon! Eventually, you will get to a point in your journey where facing every piece of you that is damaged is the much better option. My "Eventually" moment in my journey hadn't come yet. Although I had identified everything that was holding me in a broken state, I still wasn't ready to do the work. Knowing and acknowledging that I needed to look in the mirror was only half the battle. I wasn't wholeheartedly ready to take that look and do the necessary work to change what I saw. As a result, I created the "I'm okay" mask. I put on an external smile when internally I was really crying; I laughed when I was really frowning. This mask told the rest of the world I was okay when I really should have been saying "someone please, help me!" It appeared as if I was happy when I was really miserable. No one knew the weight that I carried in my heart, because I would show up in my mask ready for the day. My facade was always available to others. I became content with the lie that I was okay, and my brokenness became my identity. I was too afraid to face my issues and too lazy to be intentional about the work that it would take to reach complete wholeness. It was easier to wear the mask, to hide, and to blame everyone else for the reasons I was broken. I allowed a broken man to break the view of myself, and a dysfunctional relationship to set the standards of what I deserve. I forgot how to be happy; I lost my self-worth and self-confidence. I allowed the negative things that happened to me define who I was.

Furthermore, I permitted the negativity to hold me hostage. I was a prisoner of my insecurities, negative thoughts, anger, bitterness, and trust issues. I barely trusted God, let alone trust myself. I didn't trust God because I questioned why He would allow me to go through something as traumatic as losing a child. Why would He let me carry this child for nine months just for her to die? I didn't understand. I didn't trust myself because I always found my way into dysfunctional relationships, and I just couldn't find my way out. I blamed God; I blamed my mother and father! I blamed everybody but myself. I was okay with being the victim. When my "Eventually" came I knew something had to happen! It was life or death for me; my life was dependent upon my willingness to face myself. I was in my own way; I had the key to the prison gates. I was finally tired of me, tired of just going through the motions and pretending that I was okay and not doing the required work. It was time to commit to doing the work that was needed for me to bloom.

The process must begin; you have now entered uncharted territory! As the process is an unexplored place, you will be convinced that it is much easier to stay where you are. We know that anything worth having will take hard work and nothing will come without work. Your wholeness is worth it; the benefit of you being whole is waiting for you on the other side, and the devil will do anything to stop you from reaching your purpose in God. You will have to fight for you, fight for your freedom and your children's. The journey will create character, test your faith, patience, and self-control. In tough times is where we become intimate with GOD, but the key is to remain close when things are going well too. In this journey, you will feel empty, scared, confused, angry, and even lost. It is all part of the breakdown for the buildup. You are digging up those roots that are no longer serving you and just like uprooting a plant isn't as easy as the planting, it will take some strength and resolve. You have the keys to the gate; it is time for you to set yourself free.

Remember to trust your process and never compare your process to another's. You will get through it!

Self-reflection: Think about some parts of you that you need to face. Ask yourself why. Now, this does not mean you should sit around and ask from a defeated or victimized posture, but ask from a stance of authority. This is a spiritual dig where you must become intimate with God and yourself. Why was I attracted to broken people? You attract what you are and what you can identify with. Besides, I learned that I have a healing spirit that attracts broken people. I allowed people into my space and life, thinking I can heal and fix them, not understanding my own power.

What are some of the things that continue to keep you bound? What are those negative cycles you keep repeating? Is it your bad choice in men, the destructive habits you've created, letting your insecurities control you, allowing your anger to get the best of you, or negative self-talks? Identify everything that contributes to self-destruction. You are strong enough to face it all even when you don't feel like it. God has placed within you the strength that you need to overcome all your obstacles, including the ones we have placed in front of ourselves with our disobedient choices.

Affirmations:

I am strong and powerful.

I will remember who God says I am.

I am powerful enough to overcome my past mistakes.

God is within and around me; I am protected.

Scriptures to pull from:

Isaiah 40:29: He gives strength to the weary and increases the power of the weak.

Mark 11:24: Therefore, I tell you, whatever you ask in prayer, believe that you have received it and it will be yours.

Joshua 1:9: Have I not commanded you? Be strong and courageous. Do not be frightened, and do not be dismayed, for the Lord your God is with you wherever you go.

Write your own affirmations:

_____

_____

_____

_____

_____

_____

_____

_____

_____

_____

_____

_____

_____

_____

_____

_____

_____

_____

_____

WHO ARE YOU?

Good question. I remember when I couldn't answer this question because I had become my circumstances, and no one wants to answer this questions with, *"I am a single mother, I am dysfunction, I am insecure, controlling, and confused."* I could go on and on with the negative adjectives that became my identity. Sounds silly, right? These were exactly the thoughts I had about myself. After being in a mentally and emotionally abusive relationship, you start to allow someone else to define who you are. If you consistently hear negative things about yourself, you will begin to permit those things to manifest on the inside and outside.

For me, I started to wear dark colors—things that wouldn't bring attention to me. I was okay with not being seen or heard. After a while, the baggage becomes too heavy to carry on the inside. It starts to weigh you down and change your appearance. Think about it, you ever notice someone having an amazing day or in a very good season in life, and then you see them having a horrible day or in the middle of a storm? Usually, you can see or feel the difference.

The aftermath of my storm started to suffocate me and bury my potential, and I allowed it. As harsh as it may sound, I had to get over it all, release it, and relearn who I was meant to be. I asked myself, "Who would I be if none of these things happened to me? For me to initiate this process, I had to change my perspective of the things I had gone through—no longer making it about anyone else but me! Searching for happiness in others did not, and will never, bring the happiness that is intended for us to thrive in. That happiness can only come from knowing who you are, loving who you are, and owning your mess. So many blockades prevented me from getting to know who I truly was and establishing my internal happiness. I had to bulldoze through the past traumas to scratch the surface of the journey to true happiness and self-discovery. Your soul yearns for the type of happiness where everything and everyone else is just a bonus to you, not a necessity. Not knowing who you are and relying on someone else for your happiness will result in holding on to dead relationships longer than you should. Take me for example. I held on to a relationship that would have brought no value to my life if I were whole. If I had been truly happy with myself, I highly doubt that I would have held on to that dead situation.

Honestly, I did not understand what it meant to love myself anymore. I knew what it looked like on the surface, and I mastered the projection of self-love, but internally, I couldn't find it. My self-love journey revealed that I had some very unloving behaviors I had to dismantle. I can't believe I mistreated myself by allowing others to mistreat me. That certainly isn't self-love. Self-discovery is like pulling thorns out of your skin. It will get painful and uncomfortable, but once your soul is freed, it will feel so much better. Your wholeness is worth it!

Let's dig deep!

Imagine yourself free, secure, and strong in who you are. Who are you if you took charge of your life? Who does God say you are?

Scriptures to pull from:

2 Timothy 1:7: For God gave us a spirit not of fear but of power and love and self-control.

Philippians 4:13: I can do all things through him who strengthens me.

2 Peter 1:4: By which he has granted to us his precious and very great promises, so that through them you may become partakers of the divine nature, having escaped from the corruption that is in the world because of sinful desire.

Ephesians 1:7: In whom we have boldness and access with confidence through our faith in him.

Reflection: Take the time to think about when you allowed your circumstance to define you and why you gave your power away.

Affirmations:

I am who God says I am.

I am healing and nothing will stop that.

I am no longer a product of my environment but an overcomer of my circumstances.

I have all that I need within me…

I am responsible for my wholeness.

I am powerful.

Write your own affirmation that will help you declare who you are and who you want to become:

_____

_____

_____

_____

_____

_____

_____

_____

_____

_____

_____

_____

_____

_____

_____

_____

_____

_____

# *BREAK THE CYCLE*

What is a generational curse or cycle? Generational cycles are those habits and traits that are engraved in your DNA or learned behaviors that have been passed down generation to generation. Your mother or father did it, your grandmother or grandfather did it, and maybe your great-grandmother did it, and now, you're doing it. The effects of sin are passed down from one generation to the next. We have all heard the saying, "The apple doesn't fall too far from the tree." Typically, the statement is used to compare the looks or behavior of a child to its parents. *IT IS TIME TO BREAK THE CYCLE!* We may be carrying the sins of our parents and not know it because it is our "normal." The environment in which you were raised and who you came from will always influence your behavior until you decide to unlearn the things that no longer serve you. In order to break a cycle, you first acknowledge that an unhealthy cycle exists. I have seen so many people condemn the behaviors of their parents and then unconsciously repeat the same cycles and become unable to identify those mimicked behaviors because it is easier to look outward than inward.

Our parents or guardian(s) can only give us what they have—the good and the bad. If they are still carrying childhood or adulthood traumas, then certainly, their distorted view of life will be projected onto or engraved in you from a child. When exposed to the unhealthy habits and cycles, we acquire habits that we will later learn are hindrances to our growth in becoming all that we're meant to be. Know what you are up against, whether the cycle is lying, addictive behavior such as drug abuse, sex addiction, thieving, quitting, alcoholism, negative self-talks, low self-esteem, settling for less, or bad choices in men or women, etc. It may take initiating uncomfortable conversations with family members to understand where the cycles started and what traumas may be inducing the cycles. You are not obligated to continue to live the life that your mother or father lived. If you want better, make changes to produce better. With each generation, it can get worse and more devastating, which sheds light on how important it is for the cycle to stop with you. You are no longer living life for yourself, but also for your descendants.

Personally, I didn't realize how important this was until I had children. Being a mother changed my perspective and made me aware of cycles that needed to be broken. I couldn't imagine my daughter settling for a man that disrespected and abused her, or my son becoming a womanizer or abusive to women. It was critical that I stood up against the generational curses that were passed down, and the cycles that I was creating. My children's freedom was resting upon my shoulders and depending on my healing. The good thing is that we have the power to break the cycles. Your legacy is rooting for you and depending on your strength and determination to break those negative cycles and start positive ones. I spoke to a group of women about their generational cycles and what actions they put in place to break them. We talked about the cycle of sex addiction, codependency, and women whose parents projected the results of their childhood traumas onto them. e.g., if there was an event in your mother's life that resulted in her developing trust issues towards men, it is likely that point of view or fear will be projected onto the child, intentionally or unintentionally. As we discussed actions towards breaking cycles, here are a few I thought were helpful:

1. Distance yourself from environments that encourage the continuity of the cycles you are trying to break.

2. Hold yourself accountable and surround yourself with people who will hold you accountable for your actions. Talk to them about the cycles you are trying to break.

3. Make a better choice. We repeat cycles because we repeat the choices we make. Become self-aware of your choices. Become strategic about the choices you make.

4. Don't become ashamed of the cycles you are up against. Shame will keep you right where you are. You have the victory!

Prayer

Father God, we thank you for the strength and determination to become the best version of ourselves. We ask you to reveal the cycles that are holding us back from our full potential and after you reveal them, give us exactly what we need to break the cycles. We no longer want to operate in the space of repeated choices that keep us stagnant. Surround us with the people that will hold us accountable. Break the chains and renew our spirits. Amen!

Intentional Action: Identify any negative cycles you have inherited or started and what you are going to do to break them:

_____

_____

_____

_____

_____

_____

_____

_____

_____

Affirmation:

I am breaking the cycle of…

I will no longer allow_____ to have a hold on the coming generations or me.

I am healed from/of…

I am not my circumstances.

I am free of dysfunction.

I am whole.

I am a Queen.

I am an overcomer.

I am PEACE.

# *FINDING YOUR WAY BACK*

Finally, I'm getting back to the path I was meant to be on.

After you have gone astray—strayed from your path of purpose and allowed life to pull you away from your true essence—it is never too late to find your way back to who you're really meant to be. It is time for you to be brave and courageous, to get back to who you really are. Time to stop feeling sorry for yourself because you were the victim of something that may have emotionally, mentally, or physically scarred you. It is time for you to change your narrative. I am here to support you along the way. The journey won't be easy, and you won't like some things that may surface about yourself, but it is time to know and face your truth! You got this! Get to know yourself! Verify that you are doing this for yourself; that way, it won't be contingent upon anything or anyone other than you! Let's dig deep; let's get uncomfortable.

I was so far away from my true self that I had to relearn who I was, what I wanted, and what I deserved. My journey started when denial was no longer an option. I finally accepted that I was living in a broken place and became truthful about the depth of my brokenness—no longer ashamed of what I went through or who I had become because of it. Living my truth has commenced!

I was forced to get uncomfortable being the victim, a place I had occupied long enough to become comfortable in it. In this position, I was not allowed to grow or be free. In the victim position, I continued to replay those victimizing acts in my head which slowly but surely pulled me down into a sunken place with depression, anger, negative thoughts, and bitterness. All of these things were blocking my bloom. I gave those emotions power— the power to keep me in a mentally low place. I was finally ready to blossom, ready to be whole, and happy. My readiness was a decision I was required to make every day, hour, minute, and second, because it was so easy to fall back into the dark place. All it takes is one negative thought that I didn't control. My willingness to fight for my peace and wholeness is what kept me anchored. Are you willing to fight for you?

Identifying the things that are blocking you from reaching your full potential is the first step. I, too, had many self-inflicted blockades. Results were not possible until I was dedicated to being intentional about turning my fear into faith, my negative thoughts into positive ones, and knowing that when the negative thoughts or emotions come, I must let them pass through! In other words, I could not hold on to them and allow them to manifest and take over me. I turned the negative self-talks into positive reassurances. My affirmations remain to be a driving force, whenever I need motivation. I would say something to encourage myself, either aloud or quietly. The Lord knows I had many blocks that I put up. Sure, getting rid of the blockades is easier said than done, but necessary nonetheless! Key components for me are prayer, staying close to God, intentionally feeding my spirit the things it lacks, and surrounding myself with the right people.

I pray that every chain is broken in your life and every internal and external block crumbles. I pray that you gather the strength to let go so that you can BE!

Letting go isn't as simple as it may sound. It is an easy thought to think and an easy group of words to verbally project. Saying

"I'm going to let it go!" is a stress-relieving and enlightening statement. But if you have the ability to feel, you know that it is not that easy. It may be easy to walk in the illusion that you have let go. What I have noticed is that those who "display" ease in letting go don't realize the impact bottled-up unforgiving events and emotions have on their lives and decisions. So, what does it mean to let go? I mean, to really let go.

You've heard people say "forgive and forget." I don't think it is possible to completely forget. Just because you've forgiven doesn't mean that you will ever forget. Naturally, your brain is wired to remember, and for some reason, we definitely don't have a problem remembering the things that initiated negative emotions. Once you have decided to let go and forgive, the key is not to forget but to remain in forgiveness. If the thought of the memory still has the power to make you angry, sad, or disoriented, have you really forgiven? No, not really. Take me for example: I convinced myself that I had forgiven someone, but the mere mention of their name would bring an immediate eye roll and attitude, or the memory of hurt would automatically put a damper on my mood. The person or event was still getting a reaction from me; therefore, it was apparent I really hadn't forgiven or let go.

We are naturally emotional creatures designed to feel. Some people learn to numb themselves and store their emotions in a dark place, never addressing or releasing the emotional poison. Just like some diseases, the negativity spreads and just become "who they are." Letting go involves releasing the hold that the memory and any emotions attached to that memory have on you, not allowing it to dictate your emotions in your present moment. You can do this by acknowledging the negative emotion and let it flow out of you. This may require counseling, mantras, meditation, support groups, or journaling, and of course a lot of prayer. Whatever you do, don't shut the emotions out; bottled-up emotions will one day explode and that's a sure way to block your bloom. Instead, learn to give it to God!

Prayer is a powerful tool and learning to pray for your enemies and emotions will help you in the process. I remember when it was almost impossible for me to pray for people that hurt me or did me wrong to some degree. I would literally start praying and couldn't see the prayer through. So, instead of praying for them, I started to pray for myself: *"Father God, I have negative emotions in my heart towards_____. I am asking you to help me release and let go. I am struggling to do it on my own; I need your strength through this process. I no longer want the memory to destroy my now or have a hold on my emotions. Father, renew my thoughts, my emotions, and my heart. In Jesus' name I pray, AMEN!"* I heard a pastor say that forgiveness is spiritual, and I believe that to be true. The more I prayed for me, the more I realized that the action of forgiveness was for me, not for the other person who hurt me. To prove my point, have you ever had to forgive someone who thought they did nothing wrong or wasn't aware of their wrongdoing? You know, someone who could care less if you forgive them or not. While you're hurt or angry by their actions, they're moving on with life. By handing it over to God, you are allowing a change to take place in you. Be purposeful about giving it to GOD and doing your part in the process. When you totally let go, you give no power to people, things, or circumstances from the past or present. Stop allowing all the things that do not offer peace to have a place in your mind and heart. Pack its bags and dispose of it; no longer permit it to reside within you.

Reflection: Think about the things that you need to let go of, those things that can still get a negative emotion out of you. It may be the thought that your father left you, or that your mother wasn't there for you, or a friendship that you were betrayed in. Whatever it is, identify it.

Affirmation:

I am releasing everything that doesn't bring me peace.

I am able to forgive and move forward into bloom!

I can overcome anything that is set before me.

I allow my negative emotions to come and go without them controlling me.

I am in control of my emotions; they are not in control of me.

I will start new positive habits.

I am powerful.

I am blossoming more and more each day.

Scriptures to pull from:

Matthew 6:14: For if you forgive others of their trespasses, your heavenly Father will also forgive you…

Matthew 5:44: But I say to you, love your enemies and pray for those who persecute you…

Ephesians 4:31-32: Let all bitterness and wrath and anger and clamor and slander be put away from you, along with all malice.

[32] Be kind to one another, tenderhearted, forgiving one another, as God in Christ forgave you.

Who or what have you yet to forgive? Why are you still walking in unforgiveness?

_____

_____

_____

_____

_____

_____

_____

_____

_____

_____

_____

_____

_____

_____

_____

_____

 MIND CONTROL

Mental bondage; reoccurring negative thoughts and self-talk.

Aside from your heart, your mind is the next organ that has control. As I was in a relationship with a man who deliberately attacked my mind, he went as far as telling me, "I will mess your head up so much that no other man will ever want you." He knew if he could get to my mind, he can then completely break me. Years after the relationship was over, I was still holding on to so much of the trauma and replaying events in my head that it was stealing my joy and my life.

I didn't realize the depths of my mental bondage until I was married. My husband is a happy-go-lucky guy, pretty much always in a good mood. He tries to find the positive in all things. I, on the other hand, was the total opposite and being married to someone like that, my unhappiness was palpable. My past had won; it was controlling my now and predicting how happy I could be. You've heard the saying, "Change your thinking, change your life." Oh! This is very true. Negative thinking took up about 75% of my thoughts. My mind was the most destructive force in my life; it altered my interpretation of reality. My thoughts were self-abusive and unproductive. My negative thoughts provoked negative emotions. Negative emotions provoked negative actions. My mind was literally a battleground. I was physically released out of bondage but was mentally still living there. My thoughts were dedicated to what was done to me in my past and what I thought people were still capable of doing to me in the present. This type of thinking engendered a depressive state and zapped me of my energy every single day. The past still had power. I needed to be intentional about changing my thinking and becoming the master of my mind.

The journey of changing your thinking really takes unending intentional work. You need to accept that your negative thinking habits aren't a healthy life to live. You must find the source of the thoughts. For me, the source was not being able to let go of all that I've gone through. I permitted my negative emotions to manifest. I held everyone at the same regard as those who have hurt me. You must forgive the people who hurt you including yourself. Yes! You need to forgive yourself, too. Forgive yourself for allowing you to go through so much pain. Forgive yourself for the bad choices you've made and then apologize to yourself. Decide that negative thoughts don't deserve a place in your mind anymore.

I wish that I could tell you that changing your thinking is as easy as flipping a light switch, but it is not. You have to do the work and reprogram your mind. I can honestly tell you this was and still is the most self-work I have had to do. You are your own worst enemy; negative thoughts and self-pity won't magically disappear. Start replacing the negative thoughts with positive ones and words of affirmation. Do not let negative thoughts manifest or get comfortable in your mind. Evict them as they come; when they appear, let them go! Be mindful of what you're feeding yourself. What you read, the music you listen to, social media, and the people you choose to surround yourself with all play a part in your journey of mastering your thoughts. For me, I had to continuously read books that deposit seeds and help with my journey of positive thinking, spiritual development, and powerful thinking. As in any process, you don't start strong. You do the work and become stronger as time progress. Be patient with yourself when you have bad moments and keep fighting to be mentally free.

Affirmations:

Today, I let go of every thought that is holding me hostage to my past.

My mind is renewed, and I am free.

My positive thoughts will provoke positive emotions.

I forgive myself; I deserve a happy life filled with happy thoughts.

I am a power thinker; my thoughts provoke powerful and positive emotions for me to grow into all that God needs me to be.

Create your own affirmations and speak life over yourself daily!

_____

_____

_____

_____

_____

_____

_____

_____

_____

_____

_____

_____

_____

_____

_____

_____

_____

_____

_____

Scriptures to pull from:

Romans 12:2: And do not be conformed to this world, **but be transformed by the renewing of your mind**, so that you may prove what the will of God is, that which is good and acceptable and perfect.

2 Corinthians 10:3-5: For though we walk in the flesh, we do not war according to the flesh, for the weapons of our warfare are not of the flesh, but divinely powerful for the destruction of fortresses.

(My interpretation—we are fighting spirits that occupy the bodies, not the physical person. You will not show up to a spiritual fight the same way you'll to a physical fight. You must equip yourself accordingly).

Philippians 4:8: Finally, brethren, whatever is true, whatever is honorable, whatever is right, whatever is pure, whatever is lovely, whatever is of good repute, if there is any excellence and if anything worthy of praise, dwell on these things.

(My Interpretation—don't waste your thoughts on anything less than).

THE PURPOSE & THE PROMISE

There is power in your pain, and promise in the process! When we are in the middle of pain, we feel powerless, and in some instances, the pain consumes our very being. Your pain can be the process of discovering your real power. Everything in life is a process, and sometimes, the process is what people dislike the most. Imagine if we could skip the process and still acquire the results; I'm sure most of us would go with that option. In skipping the process, we've lost the opportunity to gain all that comes with it. The conditioning that the process brings begins to prepare us for our next level. In the process, we gain the strength, wisdom, and determination needed to sustain us at our next level. For example, a boxer trains and conditions himself for what he is about to endure. If he wants any chance at winning or lasting in the fight, he must not skip the process. If you think you can go around any process, think again! Fall in love with the process and respect the process—it is something that you can't avoid. During the process is where you will learn the most about yourself—good, bad, and indifferent. You will build your strength, peace, and faith in your process.

God already knows where you are headed and what you will need when you get there. If we pair prayer, faith, and work, then surely, all things will work together for our good. There will be lessons to learn and tests to take, and just like school, if you don't learn the lessons, you'll have to repeat the tests. This is about your growth and becoming the best version of yourself. Don't rush your development. Make sure you're "full-grown" by being patient with yourself while in the process. This isn't just for you, but also for the generations after you.

Several years after the death of my daughter, the realization was apparent that the pain I went through wasn't just for me, it was for me to make it through and help someone else get through it as well. Two other women and I came together to create Mothers In Mourning, a nonprofit organization to support mothers of angel babies. We provided them with a safe space to speak about their emotions in a room where someone could relate to the degree of pain they were feeling. Meeting with other women who have shared the same pain, listening, and being a part of their support system was the ultimate healing for me. That was a reassurance that what I went through wasn't just for me. I was strong enough to make it through and to use my strength as a small token of hope for the next woman. I was an example of God's grace! I could never just stand by and watch another woman process the loss of a child alone. Because of everything I learned in that situation, I feel obligated to support her process to the best of my ability. The pain of losing my daughter also birthed my wardrobe styling company, Twelve16, LLC. The company's name represents December 16th, in honor of her birth. This has also presented me with limitless opportunities to pour into the lives of many women. Using my experience of domestic abuse and the aftermath of it, I am able to encourage, uplift, and motivate those who are currently in the shoes I once occupied. There were purpose and promise in my pain! Of course, I couldn't see it in the midst of my pain, nor would I have ever thought I would be helping so many women through their pain. I am here to encourage you to hold on through your process, when you get through it, reach back and help someone else!

Scriptures to pull from:

Isaiah 40:29: He gives power to the weak and strength to the powerless.

2 Samuel 22:33: God is my strong fortress, and he makes my way perfect.

Romans 5:4: And endurance develops strength of character, and character strengthens our confident hope of salvation.

 BLOOM

Bloom - A flourishing, healthy condition; the time or period of greatest beauty, & artistry

Hello, Bloom! I am finally here—a place of peace, forgiveness, self-understanding, and self-mastery. As we are forever changing and blooming, life will continue to happen. We are now in bloom! How do we remain in this beautiful place that we've fought so damn hard to attain? We must maintain and continue the never-ending journey of becoming and blooming. We must continue to remind ourselves that nothing has the power to control our emotions or mind again. If for a moment we slip and allow someone to disrupt us, we must quickly get back on track. We have mastered ourselves enough to bring it back and not wallow in our own mess. By now, you know what your "mess" is. Life will constantly test you to continue to do what is needed for you to remain in bloom. It will also offer opportunities for you to apply what you have learned from previous lessons. I have failed or "semi-passed" plenty of tests, but I keep going. Give yourself credit for trying and doing your best. After all, you are human!

What does your season of bloom look like to you?

_____

_____

_____

_____

_____

_____

_____

_____

_____

_____

_____

_____

_____

_____

_____

_____

_____

_____

THE GARDENER

Let us use the analogy of a plant: You are the seed that God planted in your parents to birth. After a while, the seed becomes your responsibility. Take care of the seed; become the gardener. As the seed, you have everything you need inside of you to blossom into exactly what you're meant to be. As the gardener, it is your responsibility to ensure the seed is nurtured to bring forth a healthy bloom. A seed can only grow when it is planted in the right environment. You must consider the "soil" you're planted in, how it is nurtured, and how often you pick the weeds? In this case, the **"soil" is your environment and the things that are nurturing you. The "weeds" are the dead situations within your environment. The "roots" are those things that have manifested on the inside of you, things you've inherited and now have to manage, uproot, or unlearn.** The very first thing the gardener does is prepare the soil and plant the seed of what he wants to see manifest, and then he deliberately nurtures the environment the seed is in. He doesn't allow anything within his control to disrupt or interfere with his chances of witnessing a healthy bloom and the opportunity of seeing the seeds manifest into something beautiful. Take on a gardener's mentality and only plant the seeds of those things you would like to see manifest. Seeds can be words, actions, or thoughts. Whatever seed you plant is what you will harvest, so become fastidious about the seeds you plant and the soil that surrounds it. The seed and the soil will work together to bring forth roots.

Let's talk about your "soil." The soil provides a base for the plant's roots to hold on to as the plant grows bigger (blooms), creating stability so that the plant doesn't fall over. Nutrients in the soil help the plant grow stronger; the nutrients the plant needs are stored in the soil. The environment in which you choose to plant yourself has everything to do with how far you blossom spiritually, mentally, and emotionally. If your soil is toxic, you have placed limitations on how far you can grow within that toxic environment. Your environment is significant to the development of your life. It influences your actions, affects your mood, the way you think, and possibly your success. In bloom, you are conscious of the atmosphere you allow yourself to inhabit and of the people you allow to occupy your space. You're not planting yourself in negative thoughts, dysfunction, stagnancy, or toxic relationships—both romantic and platonic. There is a full understanding that your soil must be assessed and changed regularly, and the state of your soil will either contribute to or abate your growth. Now that I view myself as a precious seed that God planted with the intentions of blooming into something unimaginably great, I will no longer stunt my growth due to my own negligence. Clearly, I have planted myself in environments that were not conducive to my growth nor were they nurturing the seed that God planted. Therefore, I wasn't growing or developing in a way that was propelling me to my greater self.

The soil begins to nurture the seed, and roots begin to grow downward. Let's talk about your roots. There are many ways to view your roots—the dictionary describes roots as the basic cause, source or origin of something. In Chakra terms, the Root Chakra is the first of our energy centers and forms the basis and starting point for our development. However we choose to view or interpret the word *root*, it all correlates back to the start of something. Roots are the lifeline of a plant. It takes the nutrients from the soil and moves it to the leaves, and it keeps the plant anchored. A plant without strong roots will be consumed by weeds or even die. This is the perfect example of how important your environment is to the development of the roots that will grow beneath the surface. As a child, we don't have much of a say in regards to the environment that we are planted in, and as an adult, we spend a significant amount of time pulling the "weeds" of those deep-rooted fears, habits, and issues which our childhood has produced. Somewhere, I had roots of dysfunction being attracted to dysfunctional men started way before me. It was a root that grew into a weed that needed to be destroyed. Uprooting this particular weed was vital both for me and for the coming generations; it was my responsibility to save my children. In no way does this mean my children will not make their share of bad choices or mistakes. This just means I have started positive cycles and strong roots for them to inherit.

Your roots that are growing below will always become apparent on the surface. In my life, the soil of betrayal developed roots of fear which produced branches of control issues. I had this silly thought that if I could control a situation or person, I would have control over the chances of me being hurt, lied to, or the overall outcome of a situation…WRONG! The roots of denial produced branches of repeated negative cycles; the root of unforgiveness produced branches of turmoil, lack of peace, and anger. Have you ever come across someone who is unpleasant no matter what day of the week it is? It is quite possible that they are always in an unpleasant space because they have yet to consider their deepest roots, which means that they still need to uproot a number of deeply-rooted issues. Take time to uproot the weeds to make room for your true virtues to flourish. One of my favorite quotes by Ralph Waldo Emerson says, "What is a weed? A plant whose virtues have not yet been discovered." Pay attention to your soil, be cautious of the seed planted, and prune the dead branches—all of these actions are a part of your self-care. Self-care goes beyond the biweekly appointments that maintain your outer appearance. Yes, it's nice to appear that you have it all together. Many people have gotten comfortable with just appearing to be whole as we are in the age of social media which encourages us to live this way—as the representative is always present but in the depths of the person's four walls, there's a lot of inner work that needs to take place.

There is enough concentrated brokenness in the world, and we are not about that life. We know that true beauty starts within and exudes to the outer layers of our being. When I say self-care, I am referring importantly to those things that you do to take care of your mental, emotional, and spiritual self. This looks different to everyone. For me, meditation is essential to my mental and emotional self-care. I am an empath, and as such I require time to recharge. This may be spending the day alone in my own space in silence. We are spiritual beings first; if you neglect your spirit, you are neglecting yourself. Feeding your spiritual self at all times is essential to your overall well-being.

As you can see, I believe in the power of affirmations and speaking things into existence. Understanding my spiritual self helps to propel me deeper into learning and understanding to care for myself greater than what can be seen, but more so what I and those around me can feel. You may be like me and need affirmations to feed yourself self-affirming words and thoughts. I need prayer and Bible study time; these are the things that care for my spiritual self. Also, when I lack self-care, I feel it and everyone around me does too. Your spirit needs may be different from mine, so take the time to think about it and establish a self-care routine just as you've established a routine to get your hair, nails, and massages done. You belong to yourself before you belong to anyone or anything else. Fill your cup before you attempt to pour from it. You are your number one priority.

Self-reflection: *My roots are strong; I am not easily swayed.*

What are some roots that you need to uproot in order to produce a healthy bloom?

_____

_____

_____

_____

_____

_____

_____

_____

_____

_____

_____

_____

_____

_____

_____

_____

_____

Establish self-care habits that you will put in place:

_____

_____

_____

_____

_____

_____

_____

_____

_____

_____

_____

_____

_____

_____

_____

_____

_____

_____

UNDERSTANDING YOUR POWER

Power – Great or marked ability to do or act; strength; might; force. A deity; divinity: heavenly power.

Many people are caught up on the idea of being in a position of power over something or someone. You may know someone like this or this person may be you—someone who is a megalomaniac and lusts after ego-driven power. We have been trained to think this is true power, and by all means, it is a form of power. I like to call it surface power. By now, you know this book has nothing to do with anything on the surface. Let's talk about real power—true power, which you possess!

The Bible tells us that the Spirit of God dwells in us, and the first thing that God shows us is the power that we have inherited. We are shown the power of the tongue and that life and death are in the tongue (Proverbs 18:21). If you know the power you hold through the words you speak, why wouldn't you be a little more self-aware when it comes to the things you let part your lips? Your words are seeds that you plant into the universe and anything planted has the potential to grow. Don't give anything negative a chance to grow by speaking it out of your mouth. Stop using expressions like "I'll never have…", "I can't do…", and "it's just how I am…" Use your power to create the reality you desire by speaking life into yourself and everything connected to you. Use your affirmations to help you with speaking life into your situations, finances, children, spouse, and anything you want to see turnaround or manifestation.

The Power of Insight- *An understanding of the motivational forces behind one's actions, thoughts, or behavior, self-knowledge; Penetrating mental vision or discernment.* At the beginning of each year, I attend a leadership revival at a local church where Bishop T.D Jakes speaks on leadership. This particular year, he mentioned the importance of insight vs. eyesight. I knew that I was where I needed to be at the exact moment. The message was right on time; it served as a reminder for me. At the time, I was furloughed from my government job, and my husband had been laid off his job for about a month. My household had no income. With three kids, a mortgage, car payments, and a load of other bills, it was easy to become engrossed in what things looked like to the eye. I had to activate my insight. I will never forget the peace I felt during this season; my growth as a woman was apparent, and my faith in God was transparent. As a woman, who had a pattern of allowing everything to disturb my peace and rattle me, this was definitely a moment for me. Now, in all honesty, I had some moments where I slipped and started overthinking things. Those moments served as a reminder that my focus had shifted to what things looked like on the surface.

As people who are planners, my husband and I were being very strategic about saving our money; however, plans were abruptly interrupted. Watching my savings starting to deplete had the potential to send me into survival panic mode. Being aware of an issue and being fixated on it are two very different perspectives. Being aware has no control over your emotions; being fixated will give the situation power over you and your emotions. Identifying the motivational force behind my "slip-ups" definitely helped; it was fear! A part of me was afraid of the financial struggle this season could potentially bring. During my "slip-up," my awareness of the emotions and spirit that tried to overtake me was quicker than it would have been if I had not been in bloom. This could have easily turned into a downward spiral of negative emotions that I would spend days or even weeks trying to climb out of. I could have chosen stress, panic, and only focused on what my eyesight was showing me, but I chose faith instead. Remember, we always have a choice.

Activating my insight to get through this season is where my power was found and sustained. The Bible reminds us in **Proverbs 8:14– I have counsel and sound wisdom; I have insight; I have strength**. Learning the power of insight and perception has played a leading role in my ability to sustain a peaceful state. If I were to continue to allow situations and circumstances to dictate my level of peace, I would have continued to ride an emotional roller coaster. I had to take my emotions out of the driver's seat. Not only did I learn to focus on insight, but I also learned to change the way that I saw things. Yes, I had no income at the time due to the furlough, but I still had a job when it was all over. The time off gave me the opportunity to work on other businesses and put some things into perspective. Life has a way of making us either forget our power or consume us in so much malarkey that we never reach the threshold of tapping into the power we have within ourselves. Activate your power!

The Power of Vision –The Bible reminds us in Proverbs 29:18, "Where there is no vision, the people perish..." If you have no vision, where are you headed? You have to see it before you can be it. Vision is what we see and how we see it; it is your bridge from where you are to where you want to be. Envision who you want to be and where you want to go way before it actually becomes and arrives here in the physical realm. Having a vision and holding on to your vision will become an influential motivator in your life. Vision will help you create purpose for your life. Your vision will drive your decisions and if things don't align with the vision that God has given you or the one you have for yourself—gracefully walk away without apology or explanation. Vision will keep you focused on what God has promised you and what you have promised yourself. Don't ever lose focus of your vision; work towards it every day! See yourself being that multi-millionaire business owner! See yourself being an amazing mother and wife! Whatever it is that you want for yourself—envision it, practice it, study it, and be it. You will then attract those things to you.

Affirmation: Greatness and wealth are looking for me; I will plant seeds that will illuminate the trail leading directly to me.

Power Thinking- It all starts with a thought, and as I previously stated, I was a serial negative thinker. If I didn't change my thinking into power thoughts, I was certainly doomed. There is no way to obtain your purpose, power posture, or peace if a change isn't realized. Remember, as a man thinks, so is he. Your thoughts will create your reality; you will manifest the seeds you planted. That very thing that is controlling your thoughts and energy will soon appear as your reality. You have the power to think yourself into bad health, depression, negative situations, and unwanted emotions. One of my favorite quotes by James Lane Allen says, "All that a man achieves and all that he fails to achieve is the direct result of his own thoughts." Now, as a power thinker, I refuse to allow my thoughts to limit my reality or growth because I know exactly how much negative thinking will block my bloom. The good thing about the mind is that we can train and recondition it. As cliché as it may sound, after I changed my thinking, my life also started to transform. I began to attract positivity and happiness. I had a better attitude towards life. However, this did not mean that negative things stopped happening to me. It just meant the way I processed those things changed.

Don't Take It Personally- The power of taking nothing personally was a power that took me a while to activate and understand. People's attitudes and unpleasant demeanors usually have little to do with you and everything to do with them. Do any of these sound familiar to you: "Hurt people hurt people"; "Misery loves company"; or "Broken people will try to break you"? They all are sending the same message—that people will project their pain, misery, and brokenness on you. By understanding the power of not taking anything personally, you will be able to navigate your fleshly responses when dealing with these particular individuals. It may even help you to show a little empathy towards them because you know that their behavior is a reflection of their lack of bloom and underlining issues they have not yet addressed. I can recall a situation where a young lady decided to attack my character from a very hostile posture, stating things about me that I knew were not true. It was simply an opinion she conjured up in her head. My initial response was to defend my name and myself, which I did. But as I was in a combative conversation with this woman, I suddenly realized that she was projecting her insecurities and brokenness onto me. When I understood that, I instantly felt a sense of compassion. Initially, a seed of anger was planted because something untrue was being said about me, but the soil of compassion brought roots of peace which changed my posture in the situation. This had nothing to do with me; therefore, I proceeded accordingly.

I don't bother myself with baggage or battles that have nothing to do with me as I am in bloom and no longer take on another person's issues or baggage by taking things personally. Sometimes, we may be so engulfed by the present that we forget to step back and evaluate the situations we are facing to grasp that these battles we face are spiritual, not fleshly. As we acknowledge and honor the fact that we are experiencing spiritual battles, we can fight differently and more effectively. Earlier, we talked about praying for your enemies—prayer is a powerful tool. Also, understanding that negative cannot drive out negative. Only a positive can supersede a negative. Example: You can't fight anger with anger because that will equal destruction. Only compassion and love will deflate anger.

Affirmations:

I will not allow others to project their issues on to me.

I am the ruler over my emotions.

I will not give my power away.

Another person's issues are not my problem.

What others think of me is none of my business.

What does Power look like to you?

_____

_____

_____

_____

_____

_____

_____

_____

_____

_____

_____

_____

_____

_____

_____

_____

_____

_____

_____

_____

 SHE'S A VIBE

Vibe- A person's emotional state or atmosphere of a place communicated to and felt by others.

You are shifting the atmosphere when you show up. You are in bloom, and your emotional self and your spiritual self are both in the most beautiful states they have ever been. This doesn't mean that life will be free of trials and tribulations or that you won't go through anything. What it does mean is that you are responding and processing things a lot differently. Your peace is not as easily disturbed; it has become your priority. You are intentional about your self-care, what you feed your spirit, and who you let into your space. You've learned to trust yourself and listen to your intuitive power. Your presence exudes grace, peace, and light. You are nurturing and garnering greatness in abundance. You are an atmosphere shifter; your very essence carries power. You are breaking generational cycles that don't serve you well. You are trusting the process of life knowing that all things work together for your good. You are showing yourself the grace needed to continue to grow. You are empowering others with your story of triumph. You are forgiving and releasing any negative emotions that may arise in you.

You are living in full bloom!

 *AFFIRMATIONS*

I will show up for myself whole and secure.

I have the power to manifest exactly what I desire.

I am starting a positive cycle that will produce positive results.

I am full of positive loving energy; I will attract positive loving energy.

I forgive myself and set myself free.

I deserve an abundance of happiness.

My past does not define me.

Greatness is looking for me.

I radiate confidence.

I believe in myself and my ability to succeed.

I am ready for transformation.

I am brave, fearless and strong.

All things are possible, I have all that I need in this moment.

 *SCRIPTURES*

Isaiah 40:29: He gives power to the weak and strength to the powerless.

2 Samuel 22:33: God is my strong fortress, and he makes my way perfect.

Romans 5:4: And endurance develops strength of character, and character strengthens our confident hope of salvation.

2 Timothy 1:7: For God gave us a spirit not of fear but of power and love and self-control.

Philippians 4:13: I can do all things through him who strengthens me.

2 Peter 1:4: By which he has granted to us his precious and very great promises, so that through them you may become partakers of the divine nature, having escaped from the corruption that is in the world because of sinful desire.

Ephesians 1:7: In whom we have boldness and access with confidence through our faith in him.

Psalms 37:4: Take delight in the lord, and he will give you your heart's desires.

Luke 6:38: Give and it will be given unto you. A good measure, pressed down, shaken together and running over, will be poured into your lap. For with the measure you use, it will be measured to you.

2 Corinthians 1:4 Who comforts us in all out troubles, so that we can comfort those in any trouble with the comfort we ourselves receive from God.

www.Dontblockyourbloom.com

Social media handle:@Dontblockyourbloom

Made in the USA
Lexington, KY
30 October 2019